WI

Drug Legalization

A Pro/Con Issue

Jennifer Lawler

Enslow Publishers, Inc.

40 Industrial Road   PO Box 38
Box 398   Aldershot
Berkeley Heights, NJ 07922   Hants GU12 6BP
USA   UK

http://www.enslow.com

Library of Congress Cataloging-in-Publication Data

Lawler, Jennifer.
  Drug legalization : a pro/con issue / Jennifer Lawler
    p. cm. — (Hot pro/con issues)
  Includes bibliographical references and index.
  Summary: Provides an overview of legal and illegal drugs and their history of use in the United States and supporting arguments for the status quo as well as for decriminalization.
  ISBN 0-7660-1197-6
    1. Drug abuse—United States—Juvenile literature. 2. Drug legalization—United States—Juvenile literature. [1. Drug abuse. 2. Drug legalization.] I. Title. II. Series.
  HV5825.L378   1999
  364.1'77—dc21   98-34043
                                                      CIP
                                                      AC

Printed in the United States of America

10 9 8 7 6 5 4 3 2 1

To Our Readers:
All Internet addresses in this book were active and appropriate when we went to press. Any comments or suggestions can be sent by e-mail to Comments@enslow.com or to the address on the back cover.

Illustration Credits:
AP/Wide World Photos, pp. 14, 31, 38, 40, 42, 48, 54; National Archives, pp. 1, 4, 8.

Cover Illustration: Corbis-Digital Stock

Contents

Introduction

Sam,* a high school student, always looked up to Eric, his sister Melissa's boyfriend. Eric frequently came to dinner at Sam's house. Sometimes, he even stayed the night. Because Sam felt like an outsider in his small Massachusetts town, Eric's friendship meant a lot to him.

One night, Eric asked Sam to meet him at the campus of a nearby college. He bought Sam a beer. Then, he asked whether Sam could find him some marijuana. Sam did not want to do it. But Eric had always been nice to him, so he agreed. While Eric waited, Sam went to an acquaintance and got the marijuana. He sold it to Eric for twenty dollars.

Then, Eric said he was working undercover for the police. Sam was arrested and prosecuted. Although this was his first offense, and he was a minor, he was sentenced to ten years in prison. The reason for the long sentence? He had sold drugs in a school zone.

When Eric testified at the trial, he was asked whether he had cared about Melissa, Sam's sister. Eric laughed and said he would never be interested in a girl like that.

Sam's lawyer was outraged. So were his family and the community. As one observer said, the police officer

> was paid to become intimate with a young woman to gain the trust of her younger brother.

*real names not used

[He was paid] to encourage a minor to drink alcohol. The department paid him to arrange a transaction close to the college to increase Sam's sentence under a law designed to protect elementary school children from drug dealers. Except in this case, the law served to incarcerate [jail] a kid who is younger than the attendees of the nearby school. Since when is this the proper role of law enforcement?[1]

Although many people objected, Sam is currently serving his sentence at a bootcamp facility operated by the Massachusetts Department of Corrections.

▼ ▼ ▼

A case such as this one involves many of the reasons some people believe that drugs should be legalized. The case involved an extreme penalty for a first-time offender, who was also a minor. It involved the unnecessary harm to an innocent person (Melissa). And it involved the cost of using a

Marijuana

- About 11 million Americans age twelve and over currently use marijuana.
- Seventy-seven percent of current illegal drug users use marijuana.
- More than one half of young people age twelve to seventeen reports that marijuana is easy to obtain.

Source: The National Household Survey on Drug Abuse, conducted by the Substance Abuse and Mental Health Services Administration, 1997.

police officer to trap an otherwise law-abiding citizen. People who support drug legalization say all these things are wrong.

But a recent poll showed that an overwhelming majority of Americans (about 95 percent) think there is a serious drug problem.[2] Most people agree that the current drug policy is not working very well. Although there are harsh penalties for drug crimes, they have not stopped people from using or dealing drugs.

Some individuals believe that the drug laws should not change. They say current laws will work. Over time, fewer people will abuse drugs. Other people think that the drug policy should be even tougher. They think that there should be longer prison sentences and more money should be spent on increasing law enforcement.

Still others believe that the whole system is misguided. Many of these people believe that drug addicts have a medical problem. They should not be treated like criminals. Others say that using drugs such as marijuana for medical reasons should not be punished. Some people also think

Trends in Drug Use					
1992	1993	1994	1995	1996	1997
Monthly Use of Drugs for Eighth Graders					
7%	9%	11%	13%	15%	13%
Monthly Use of Drugs for Tenth Graders					
11%	14%	17%	19%	23%	23%
Monthly Use of Drugs for Twelfth Graders					
14%	17%	21%	24%	25%	26%

Source: Department of Health and Human Services, Public Health Service. National Survey Results on Drug Use, from the Monitoring the Future Study, 1998.

that using marijuana or other drugs for recreation should not be punished, either. According to a 1997 survey, 35 percent of all college freshmen believed marijuana should be legal.[3]

These different points of view make up the drug legalization debate. Where do these conflicting opinions come from? How can each group feel so strongly about its opinions? Although there are no easy answers, a decision can only be made after considering both sides of drug legalization.

While many Americans think current drug laws should be even tougher, other people think that some drugs, like marijuana (pictured), should be legalized.

Chapter 1

Drugs of Abuse

The word *drugs* means different things to different people. To doctors and pharmacists, it means medications used to treat diseases. To police officers, it means illegal substances that alter a person's moods, feelings, and personality.

Drug Misuse and Abuse

How can something that has good qualities also be so bad? It depends on how a drug is used. Therapeutic drug use helps people. Drug misuse or abuse harms people.

Drug misuse happens when a drug is used in a way that was not meant. For example, a person might use pain medication to feel good, not to control pain. *Drug abuse* happens when a person feels he or she *must* use a drug, regardless of the consequences.

Sometimes drug abuse occurs when a person taking a drug for a medical reason overuses it or uses it after it is no longer needed. This happens with pain-killers, such as codeine, and depressants, such as Valium.

Other legal drugs, such as tobacco and alcohol, can also be abused. However, there is no medical reason to use these drugs. Illegal drugs, such as heroin and cocaine, are also abused by people who have no medical reason to take them.

Why do people misuse and abuse drugs? One reason is that drugs can make a person "high." A high is a sense of feeling good, of being happy. Another reason is to fit in with friends who use drugs. Sometimes people use drugs to forget their other problems. Drugs are misused for other reasons, too. Some athletes misuse steroids to increase their strength and body weight. Steroid abuse is very dangerous, because it can cause liver damage, high blood pressure, aggressive behavior, and other problems.[1]

Almost 14 million Americans abuse or misuse drugs. Estimates suggest that at least one out of every ten drug users will end up with a serious problem, which is cause for concern. It is why the government makes rules about using drugs.[2]

Drug Schedules and Classifications

To guide people in using drugs appropriately, the federal government classifies drugs into groups, called *schedules*. There are five schedules of drugs. Schedule I drugs are the most addictive and the most dangerous, according to the government. Schedule V drugs are the least dangerous. The drugs of abuse that cause the most concern are Schedule I and Schedule II drugs which include heroin and cocaine. Drugs are also classified by their effects on

Drugs Classified by Schedule

Schedule I

Drug has a high potential for abuse.	Drug has no currently accepted medical use in treatment in the U.S.*	Lack of safety for use of the drug under medical supervision.	Drugs include heroin, LSD, marijuana, and methaqualone.

Schedule II

Drug has a high potential for abuse.	Drug has a currently accepted medical use in treatment in the U.S.	Abuse of drug may lead to severe psychological or physical dependence.	Drugs include morphine, PCP, cocaine, and methadone.

Schedule III

Drug has less potential for abuse than Schedule I and II drugs.	Drug has a currently accepted medical use in treatment in the U.S.	Abuse of the drug may lead to moderate physical or high psychological dependence.	Drugs include anabolic steroids, aspirin with codeine, and some sedatives.

Schedule IV

Drug has less potential for abuse than Schedule I and II drugs.	Drug has a currently accepted medical use in treatment in the U.S.	Abuse of the drug may lead to limited physical or psychological dependence.	Drugs include sedatives and narcotics, such as Darvon, Equanil, Valium, and Xanax.

Schedule V

Drug has a low potential for abuse compared with drugs in Schedule IV.	Drug has a currently accepted medical use in treatment in the U.S.	Abuse of the drug may lead to limited physical or psychological dependence.	Over-the-counter cough medicine with codeine.

*Although marijuana is a Schedule I drug, it is believed to have some medicinal value and several states have made it legal for medical use.

the body, such as depressants, stimulants, and hallucinogens. These classifications help people understand the physical effects of drugs, as well as their risks.

Drugs that are illegal or require a prescription are called controlled substances, because there are laws regarding their use, possession, and sale. Drugs that can be bought by anyone without a prescription are called over-the-counter medications. Common over-the-counter medications include cold medicines, aspirin, and cough syrups. Although these drugs may have side effects, such as drowsiness or excitability, they are considered the least dangerous drugs of all and are unlikely to cause addiction. However, it is possible to overdose on or have a fatal reaction to an over-the-counter medication.

Addictive Drugs

Addictive drugs can cause psychological or physical dependence. *Psychological dependence* means a person thinks he or she needs the drug to feel better. *Physical dependence* means the body relies on the drug and will have physical symptoms, such as muscle tremors or insomnia, if the drug is no longer used. *Withdrawal symptoms* are the physical effects that occur after a person stops using a drug. They include tension, fear, sleeplessness—even seizures and hallucinations. Sometimes withdrawal symptoms can be life-threatening. Drug *tolerance* means the user needs more and more of a drug to get the same effect from it.[3]

Addiction, sometimes called drug *dependency*, is the loss of control over the use of a drug. It means continuing to use a drug even after bad results or consequences. Addiction can include psychological

Drug Classifications by Effect

Type	Uses	Effects	Length of Effect	Risks and Consequences	Examples
Narcotics	Relieve pain, cause numbness, and induce sleep	Happiness followed by sleepiness	About six hours	Loss of appetite, physical dependence, withdrawal symptoms, possible death	Includes drugs made from opium, such as heroin, codeine, and morphine
Depressants (also called sedatives and tranquilizers)	Relax the body and reduce body functions	Calm and tranquillity	Four to twelve hours	Confusion, depression, physical and psychological dependence, possible death	Seconal, Valium, alcohol, Librium, and phenobarbital; "Special K," an animal tranquilizer, is becoming popular
Stimulants	Excite or energize the body, sometimes used to treat mental disorders	Alertness, talkativeness, activity, and other signs of excitement	Several minutes to a few hours, depending on the drug used	Irritability, confusion, sleeplessness, physical dependence, withdrawal symptoms, possible death	Mild forms found in some sodas, chocolate, tobacco, and coffee; also cocaine and amphetamines
Hallucinogens	Alter perception	Exhilaration, anxiety, and excitement; may see or hear things that are not there	Four to twenty-four hours; some effects may be permanent (flashbacks, panic attacks)	Hallucinations, paranoia, and psychosis (loss of contact with reality)	Peyote, LSD, and PCP
Designer Drugs	Synthetic drugs that mimic street-drug effects	Excitement and exhilaration	Up to several hours, depending on type	Hallucinations, paranoia, even death	Methamphet-amine, Nexus, Fantasia, and Ecstasy

Source: David E. Larson, M.D., ed., *Mayo Clinic Family Health Book* (New York: William Morrow, 1990), pp. 436–443.

dependence, physical dependence, or both. People with drug dependency, often called *addicts*, can suffer many problems. They may stop caring about themselves, their families, and their friends. They may stop caring about their jobs and their school-work. Even if they want to stop using drugs, often they cannot.[4]

Other Drugs

Different products and chemicals can also be used to get high. One example is inhalants. Inhalants are chemicals that people sniff, such as spray paint. Users spray a can of paint into a paper bag and then inhale or "huff" it to get high. Glue and nail polish

*A*lcohol, a depressant, can be just as addictive and damaging as illegal drugs. Four Vermont teens were killed in this car on their way back home from Québec, Canada, after a night of drinking.

can also be misused in this way. Inhaling such products can cause heart, liver, and kidney problems—even death. Headaches, dizziness, and coughing can last for a long time after use.[5]

Other drugs are misused and abused. Steroids, for example, have legitimate medical uses. But sometimes they are used illegally by athletes to increase body strength and endurance. Steroid users can develop problems such as hair loss and breast changes as well as liver and heart damage. Steroid use can cause aggressive and even violent behavior. These so-called 'roid rages make a user act in a way he or she normally would not.[6]

Recently, many athletes have been misusing Sudafed®, a popular decongestant. They use it to get more energy before a performance. Often they take several times the recommended dosage.

Sources estimate that 20 percent of all professional hockey players misuse this drug. Some players report that it causes users to get "hyped up." They act more aggressively and with less regard for physical safety. One hockey player says, "You get pretty wired up. Sometimes it gets you a little emotional on the ice, a little too fired up." Users also believe they build a tolerance to the drug.[7]

Pseudoephedrine, the active ingredient in Sudafed®, increases lung capacity by unblocking sinuses. It also raises the heart rate and blood pressure. Side effects include tremors and anxiety. Although not physically addictive, this drug might cause psychological dependency.[8]

Legal Drugs of Abuse

Some harmful drugs that have no medical use are legal. Some, such as caffeine, are not as dangerous

Effects of Legal Drugs

Type	Drug Classification	Effects	Risks and Consequences	Examples
Caffeine	Stimulant	Excitement, exhilaration	Irritability, sleeplessness; increases heart rate and blood pressure; may increase risk of cancer, breast disease, and birth defects; may cause mild physical dependence	Coffee, some soft drinks, and chocolate
Alcohol	Depressant	Muscle relaxation, reduces body function	Can cause aggression and paranoia; can alter perception; affects reflexes and judgment; can cause brain damage, liver damage, and psychosis (loss of contact with reality)	Beer, wine, wine coolers, and hard liquor
Tobacco (nicotine)	Stimulant	Excitement, exhilaration	Increases heart rate and blood pressure; can cause heart disease, cancer, birth defects, and many other diseases; physical and psychological dependence are common; withdrawal symptoms; "second-hand" smoke affects non-smokers adversely	Cigarettes, cigars, snuff, and chewing tobacco

as others, such as alcohol and tobacco products. Caffeine is found in certain grocery products that can be purchased by anyone. Alcohol and tobacco products are legal drugs that any adult can readily obtain. But they all have mental and physical risks.

More than one-half million deaths in the United States each year are directly caused by alcohol and tobacco use. Alcohol use costs taxpayers and employers $86 billion every year, and tobacco use costs $65 billion. These figures include expenses for prosecuting drunk drivers; medical costs associated with treating cancer and other diseases related to tobacco or alcohol use; days lost from work; and other economic losses. In comparison, illegal drug use causes fewer than ten thousand deaths each year. Less than $60 billion is lost because of illegal drug use. This figure includes the cost of law enforcement and imprisonment. However, if such drugs were made legal, the cost in tax dollars and human lives would rise to levels similar to those of alcohol and tobacco use.[9]

Chapter 2

History of Drugs and Drug Use

Drugs have been used throughout history for a variety of reasons. In addition to medical uses, drugs have been taken for recreational purposes. A recreational purpose is when a drug is used for fun—to get high or to feel good. Opium was smoked all over the world as a recreational drug during the eighteenth and nineteenth centuries.[1]

But other uses of drugs have been important, too. American Indians have traditionally used peyote (a type of dried cactus) during religious ceremonies. Peyote can cause an altered state of mind. This was thought to lead to enlightenment. Today, some American Indian groups are still allowed to use peyote during their rituals.

Drug Use in the United States

In the nineteenth century, American companies made and sold habit-forming drugs such as morphine and heroin. No prescription was needed. A person could go to any grocery store and buy products containing drugs, such as McMunn's Elixir of Opium. Another popular tonic, called laudanum, also contained opium. It was used to treat stress, nervous disorders, and depression. It was readily available to any adult or child.

During this time, cocaine was used to treat opium, morphine, and alcohol addiction, because no one knew that it was also an addictive drug. Even Coca-Cola contained cocaine during the early twentieth century. The drink was sold as a tonic to treat medical problems. Cocaine and products containing cocaine were even sold door-to-door.[2]

Early Attempts to Regulate Drug Use

As drug use and abuse became more widespread, people began committing crimes to support their habits. By the late nineteenth century, drug use had become a cause for concern. Politicians made laws that restricted the use and sale of habit-forming substances. The first of these laws was the Pure Food and Drug Act of 1906. It required any product that contained opium or cocaine, or similar substances, to be labeled. This helped consumers be aware of what they were buying.

The Pure Food and Drug Act was successful in reducing the sale of such medicines. Once people were aware of the addictive drugs in popular products, they did not want to use them.[3] Other laws, such as the Harrison Narcotics Act of 1914, prohibited the use and sale of narcotics except for medical reasons. Over time, such drug control laws reduced the availability of addictive drugs.[4]

In 1919 the Volstead Act, along with the Eighteenth Amendment to the Constitution, outlawed the manufacture, transportation, use, and sale of alcohol. This was part of a reform movement that swept the United States at the end of World War I. The Eighteenth Amendment, called the prohibition amendment, did not work as intended. Illegal clubs, called speakeasies, opened. Members could purchase "bootleg" (illegal) alcohol. People were sickened and even killed by drinking illegally produced alcohol that poisoned them. The manufacture of illegal alcohol, which could be a dangerous process, also injured and killed people. Organized crime groups controlled the distribution of alcohol. They earned huge profits on illegal trade. They committed many terrible crimes to control this trade.

Prohibition was repealed in 1933. However, the failure of the Prohibition Era did not stop the government from banning other substances. In 1937 marijuana was made illegal.[5] It had been grown by American farmers for generations. It was used to make rope, canvas, paper, and cloth. Even so, the dangers of the drug were thought to outweigh the benefits of the plant.

There are 11 million alcohol drinkers under the age of twenty-one in the United States. Of these, almost 4.5 million are binge drinkers, including 1.9 million heavy drinkers.

Source: The National Household Survey on Drug Abuse, conducted by the Substance Abuse and Mental Health Services Administration, 1997.

By the 1960s recreational drug use was again on the upswing. Historians suggest several reasons for this increased drug use. During this time of social upheaval, young people used drugs to rebel against a restrictive society. Young adults no longer had personal knowledge of the dangers of drug use, as people of earlier generations had.[6] In the 1960s and early 1970s, drugs such as marijuana and heroin were readily available to soldiers fighting in Vietnam. Half of them reported using drugs other than marijuana, and 25 percent became addicted to a drug during their military service. As the soldiers returned from Vietnam, they brought drugs and drug problems with them.

Over the next several years efforts were made to stop drug use, including harsher penalties, drug treatment (sometimes forced), and education and prevention efforts.

In the 1980s, the costs of drug abuse to individuals and to society became so great that people demanded stronger measures to stop drug use and drug dealing. This new "get-tough" attitude led to the federal government's so-called War on Drugs.

Chapter 3

The War on Drugs

In 1971, President Nixon declared that drugs were "America's Public Enemy Number One."[1] The Drug Enforcement Administration (DEA) was established in 1973 to control illegal trafficking of drugs. But it was only in the 1980s that the government began to massively fund the enforcement of drug laws. Responding to public pressure, the government created strict new laws about drug use. This "war on drugs" began in 1982 when President Ronald Reagan called for stronger laws and increased law enforcement.[2]

To further control drug use, the Anti-Drug Abuse Act of 1986 became law. Its main focus was mandatory sentencing. Under these guidelines a drug offender must serve a minimum number of years in jail. A mandatory sentence is required even for first offenses, regardless of the circumstances. Minimum prison sentences are required even if the amount of drug involved is small. For instance, the mandatory sentence for possession of one gram of LSD is five years in jail.[3] A gram is about the size of a jelly bean.

In 1989, alarmed that millions of people still used

drugs, President George Bush officially began his war on drugs. He called for an $8 billion budget. Most of this money was spent on law enforcement efforts. It was used to build jails, hire police officers, and appoint judges. Only a small amount was allotted for prevention, education, and treatment.[4]

The war on drugs preoccupied President Bush. It remained an important concern after President Bill Clinton was elected in 1992. Many of the strict laws that are a result of the war on drugs still exist.

Results of the War on Drugs

In some ways this war on drugs worked. In 1989, the National Institute on Drug Abuse reported that drug use had declined among casual users by almost 40 percent over the previous ten years. Cocaine use declined by more than 20 percent.[5] However, millions of Americans still used drugs. Some drug use increased, particularly among the poor and among teens. The number of high school seniors who said that they had used marijuana in the past year at least once declined from a high of 54 percent

Drug Availability

- One quarter of young people age twelve to seventeen report that heroin is easy to obtain.
- Fifteen percent of young people report being approached by someone selling drugs in the past month.

Source: The National Household Survey on Drug Abuse, conducted by the Substance Abuse and Mental Health Services Administration, 1997.

in 1985 to 48 percent in 1997. But the number of high school seniors who said they had tried LSD at least once increased by more than 75 percent, from 7.5 percent in 1985 to 13 percent in 1997.[6]

For these reasons, many people considered the war on drugs unsuccessful. Critics point to several problems. One was the lack of money for treatment, education, and research. Without money for research, scientists cannot learn about ways to treat addiction. Without treatment programs, addicts continue to use drugs regardless of the penalties. Without education, new users misuse and abuse drugs each year.[7]

Problems also arose when states were expected to enforce strict federal laws without having the money to do so. Laws of forfeiture allowed the confiscation of the property of people engaged in drug offenses. These laws drew criticism from citizens and lawyers. Usually, cars and money were confiscated, but other property could be, too. The worst criticism of forfeiture was that it did not require a conviction—or even a trial. Assumption of guilt goes against the Constitution, which says that

Alcohol, Tobacco, and Illegal Drug Use Among High School Seniors, 1975–1997

Percentage Ever Used											
	1975	1980	1985	1990	1991	1992	1993	1994	1995	1996	1997
Alcohol	90.4	93.2	92.2	89.5	88.0	87.5	87.0	80.4	80.7	79.2	81.7
Tobacco	73.6	71.0	68.8	64.4	63.1	61.8	61.9	62.0	64.2	63.5	65.4
Illegal Drugs	55.2	65.4	60.6	47.9	44.1	40.7	42.9	45.6	48.4	50.8	54.3

Source: Monitoring the Future, University of Michigan and the National Institute on Drug Abuse, 1998.

Drug-Related Arrests

- Yearly Total of All Arrests: 15,168,100
- Drug-Abuse Violations: 1,506,200
- Driving Under the Influence: 1,467,300
- Liquor-Law Violations: 677,400
- Drunkenness: 718,700

Source: FBI, Uniform Crime Reports, 1996.

people are innocent until proven guilty. But property confiscation helped states pay for the federal government's war on drugs, so it was used throughout the country.[8]

The sudden increase in arrests could not be supported by the jails or the courts. Drug arrests rose from about fifty-five thousand in 1985 to almost ninety-five thousand in 1989. Casual drug users were penalized the same as drug dealers. Since jails were overcrowded, people served shortened sentences. Dealers and traffickers were soon back on the streets. Violent offenders, such as rapists and murderers, were also given reduced sentences to make room for drug dealers.

In New York City, prison overcrowding became so bad that officials were forced to use jail boats. Then city officials decided to change their focus. They began to spend their time and money on catching dealers and traffickers, not users. Prison overcrowding was quickly relieved. Court and

Percentage of Students Who Report Using Drugs

Drug	Grade	Annual Use		Monthly Use	
		1996	1997	1996	1997
Cigarettes (nicotine)	Jr. High	49.2	47.3	21.0	19.4
	Sr. High	61.2	60.2	30.4	29.8
	12th	63.5	65.4	34.0	36.5
Any Alcohol	Jr. High	46.5	45.5	26.2	24.5
	Sr. High	65.0	65.2	40.4	40.1
	12th	72.5	74.8	50.8	52.7
Marijuana	Jr. High	18.3	17.7	11.3	10.2
	Sr. High	33.6	34.8	20.4	20.5
	12th	35.8	38.5	21.9	23.7
Cocaine	Jr. High	3.0	2.8	1.3	1.1
	Sr. High	4.2	4.7	1.7	2.0
	12th	4.9	5.5	2.0	2.3
Uppers	Jr. High	9.1	8.1	4.6	3.8
	Sr. High	12.4	12.1	5.3	5.5
	12th	9.5	10.2	4.0	4.8
Downers	Jr. High	3.3	2.9	1.5	1.2
	Sr. High	4.6	4.9	1.7	2.2
	12th	4.6	4.7	2.0	1.8
Inhalants	Jr. High	12.2	11.8	5.8	5.6
	Sr. High	9.5	8.7	3.3	3.0
	12th	7.6	6.7	2.5	2.5
Hallucinogens	Jr. High	4.1	3.7	1.9	1.8
	Sr. High	7.8	7.6	2.8	3.3
	12th	10.1	9.8	3.5	3.9
Heroin	Jr. High	1.6	1.3	0.7	0.6
	Sr. High	1.2	1.4	0.5	0.6
	12th	1.0	1.2	0.5	0.5
Designer Drugs	Jr. High	2.3	2.3	1.0	1.0
	Sr. High	4.6	3.9	1.8	1.3
	12th	4.6	4.0	2.0	1.6
Any Illegal Drug	Jr. High	23.6	22.1	14.6	12.9
	Sr. High	37.5	38.5	23.2	23.0
	12th	40.2	42.4	24.6	26.2

Source: Parents' Resource Institute for Drug Education (PRIDE)

prison costs were dramatically reduced. However, this approach was not completely successful, because trafficking and dealing are much more difficult to control than possession and use.[9]

Some states began to focus on education and prevention efforts by using programs such as Drug Abuse Resistance Education (DARE). However, it is unclear how effective such programs are. In 1991, the National Institute on Drug Abuse reported that there was no difference in drug use between those who had participated in a DARE program and those who had not. Subsequent reports showed that some students who had participated in a DARE program had higher rates of drug use. For these reasons, DARE and similar programs have come under heavy criticism. Some people believe such programs can actually make children interested in drugs.[10]

Currently, the government approach is set by the Office of National Drug Control Policy. The office was established by an act of Congress in 1988. It targets four main areas: treatment, prevention, law enforcement, and interdiction (stopping drug trafficking).

Mario Cuomo, the former governor of New York State, explains how this approach works. Cuomo is now a cochairperson for an antidrug organization called the Partnership for a Drug-Free America. "You must use tough laws against drug dealers," he says,

> You must interdict [stop traffickers] at the border and surely you must treat addicts. But you also must educate people, as young as possible, not to try drugs. We simply must cut demand for these "products." If we're serious about preventing drug use, we must use the most powerful tools at our disposal, including mass media.[11]

Chapter 4

Terms and Concepts of the Drug Legalization Debate

Even though efforts have been made to stop drug abuse, millions of people still use drugs. As a result, some people question the wisdom of spending more time and money enforcing drug laws that do not work. These individuals believe that the legalization of drug use is one of the ways to reduce the costs of drug use to society. Because current laws do not stop the problem, those laws should be changed.

However, opponents of legalization believe that problems of drug use would become much greater if drugs were legalized. Both sides of the legalization debate agree that drug abuse is a dangerous problem. They just do not agree on how to fix the problem. In order to understand the debate over legalization and to understand what the different sides think should be done, it is important to understand some key terms and concepts.

Approaches to Drug Legalization

There are several different approaches to legalizing drugs. The most extreme position says that all drugs should be legal because adults have a right to do as they wish with their bodies. Supporters of this position say it is wrong for the government to tell them what they can and cannot do with their own bodies in their own homes as long as they are not harming others. They say that people engage in other destructive or addictive behaviors, and the government does not try to stop them. Why should the government ban drugs just because some people become addicted to them?

People who believe that drugs should be freely available usually agree that there should be certain restrictions designed to protect others, such as not driving while under the influence of a drug. But not very many people believe that all drugs should be bought and sold freely. Most believe that some restrictions on drug sales should apply. Many supporters of legalization believe that soft drugs, such as marijuana, should be made legal, whereas hard drugs, such as crack cocaine, should remain illegal. Drug control efforts should concentrate on hard drugs.

Decriminalization

One approach to drug legalization is *decriminalization*, which means allowing people to have and use small quantities of a drug for themselves. While drug dealing and drug trafficking would remain illegal, drug users would not be punished. The idea is that education and prevention can help people stay away from drugs. Under decriminalization, a person caught with a small amount of drugs is simply fined, much like being caught for speeding in a car. Eleven states currently treat possession of marijuana in this way. It is called a "civil" offense, not a "criminal" offense. In these eleven states (Alaska, California, Colorado, Maine, Minnesota, Mississippi, New York, Nebraska, North Carolina, Ohio, and Oregon), after marijuana was decriminalized, there was an initial increase in marijuana use. But then, the number of people who reported marijuana use declined.[1]

Harm Reduction

Many people support legalization in the form of *harm reduction*. They believe that a certain number of people will abuse drugs no matter what. The best way to deal with this is to control the amount of harm that drug use causes. For example, heroin users who inject heroin are at a high risk for contracting acquired immunodeficiency syndrome (AIDS). This disease is passed from one person to another through bodily fluids such as blood. It can be contracted by sharing needles. Harm reduction supporters say that clean needles should be provided to drug users. This way, the harm of heroin use is not made worse by the harm of contracting AIDS.

Heroin users can also be given methadone, a drug that satisfies the craving for heroin without creating a high (an artificial feeling of happiness). Withdrawal from heroin is then possible, although the user becomes addicted instead to methadone. Methadone is a much less dangerous drug than heroin. A methadone user can get and keep a job.

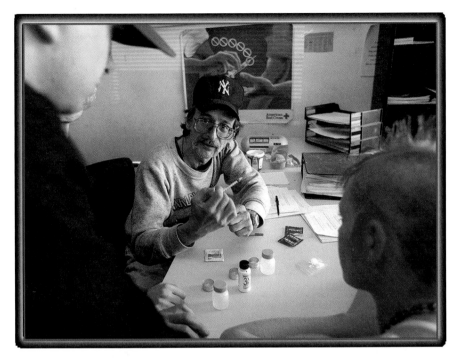

*H*ere, a worker at a needle exchange program shows two people how to clean needles with water and bleach.

He or she can lead an otherwise fairly normal life, unlike a true heroin addict.[2]

Medicalization

Some supporters of drug legalization believe that instead of allowing drug use to be simply tolerated or freely legalized, it should be regulated with the help of the medical community. This is called *medicalization.* What it means is that doctors would be allowed to prescribe illegal drugs for patients who are already addicted to them. In the best of circumstances, this would be part of a treatment program. Even if addicts never stopped using the drug, they would not turn to crime to support their habit. It would also prevent users from getting contaminated drugs that could be even more harmful to them. Such an approach could reduce overdoses and accidental deaths related to drug use.[3]

Experiences of Other Countries

Other countries have experimented with different degrees of legalization. The results are often used to strengthen the case for or against drug legalization in this country. Different countries have tried various approaches, but most have concentrated on programs aimed at harm reduction.

Harm Reduction. Poland, the United Kingdom, Denmark, and France are among the countries that have instituted needle exchange programs. To reduce the spread of infectious diseases, such as AIDS, drug users who inject themselves should always use clean needles. Needle exchange programs allow users to trade old, used needles for new, clean needles. This reduces the risk of infectious disease. Critics of such programs say they simply encourage and condone drug use.[4]

For addicts who are trying to quit using heroin, some countries have tried methadone maintenance. Methadone acts like heroin, although it is not as dangerous. It is believed that allowing the use of methadone will encourage addicts to quit heroin. Methadone maintenance is allowed in countries such as Spain, Ireland, Denmark, and Austria as well as the United States.[5]

In the United Kingdom and Switzerland, medicalization is allowed. Doctors routinely prescribe illegal drugs to addicts to reduce the amount of harm drug abuse causes.[6] In addition to prescribing only maintenance doses of relatively pure drugs, doctors counsel these patients on how to quit using drugs.

International Figures on Hard Drug Use

Country	Number of Addicts	Inhabitants (Millions)	Per 1,000 of Population
Austria	10,000	7.8	1.3
Belgium	17,500	10.0	1.8
Denmark	10,000	5.1	2.0
France	135,000/150,000	57.0	2.4/2.6
Germany	100,000/120,000	79.8	1.3/1.5
Greece	35,000	10.1	3.5
Ireland	2,000	3.5	0.6
Italy	175,000	57.8	3.0
Luxembourg	2,000	0.4	5.0
The Netherlands	25,000	15.1	1.6
Norway	4,500	4.3	1.0
Portugal	45,000	10.0	4.5
Spain	120,000	39.4	3.0
Sweden	13,500	8.6	1.6
Switzerland	26,500/45,000	6.7	4.0/6.7
United Kingdom	150,000	57.6	2.6

Source: World Health Organization Regional Office for Europe, 1994.

Decriminalization. Some countries have decriminalized the personal use of drugs, which means that people are not jailed for possessing and using small quantities of a drug. Spain and the Czech Republic have decriminalized drug use. Mostly this pertains to soft drugs such as marijuana. These countries focus their efforts on prevention and education as opposed to punishment. In Spain the personal use of drugs is not punished and has not been since 1973. In 1988, laws were reformed to help strengthen the goal of prevention, not prosecution. In the Czech Republic, although use has been decriminalized, users still tend to hide their habits out of a fear of prosecution.[7]

Effects of Harm Reduction and Decriminalization. Needle exchange programs, methadone maintenance programs, and decriminalization have existed in some countries for more than ten years. For the most part, no clear conclusions can be drawn. In the United Kingdom the number of addicts using intravenous (IV) drugs, which are injected into the body with a needle, has declined. So has the rate of AIDS infection. However, in Spain, which decriminalized personal drug use, the rate of drug use—especially that of heroin and cocaine—has increased. Treatment for addicts in treatment centers and emergency rooms has also increased.[8]

Drug Policy in the Netherlands. Supporters of drug legalization often point to the Dutch policy on drug use. The Netherlands has perhaps the most liberal drug use policy of any nation. The law distinguishes between traffickers and users. Traffickers are dealt with harshly, whereas users are not prosecuted, except in relation to prosecuting a drug trafficker. Methadone treatment is readily available to heroin users, and needles are easily obtained, usually for free. The main effort is to prevent drug abuse and treat drug users.

One of the results of this emphasis is a concern with distinguishing between hard and soft drugs. Because soft drugs are not considered as dangerous as hard drugs, the government allows the retail sale of marijuana. Officials in the Netherlands believe that many young people will want to try soft drugs. If they keep the market for soft and hard drugs separate, they are more likely to prevent young people from trying harder drugs. For this reason, "coffee shops" have sprung up all over the Netherlands, where marijuana can be legally obtained and used. Such coffee shops are tolerated so long as they follow three rules: They cannot sell to anyone younger than eighteen, they cannot advertise, and they cannot sell hard drugs.

About 6 percent of the population uses marijuana, a number that has remained the same throughout the 1990s. (The percentage is about three times as high in the United States.) The number of hard drug addicts has stayed the same as well, with few drug-related deaths reported. The number of heroin users is very low and has fallen in recent years. Crack cocaine has not appealed to the Dutch either. Allowing the use of soft drugs in the Netherlands seems to have controlled the wide-spread use of hard drugs. The idea of marijuana being a stepping-stone to other drugs seems to hold true only when marijuana and harder drugs are available together. Some officials believe that the lack of repression allows young people to see the consequences of hard drug use without thinking of it as a form of social expression or rebellion.[9]

According to the European Communities Report on Drug Demand Reduction, the number of hard drug addicts in the Netherlands is about 1.6 per 1,000 people. This is much lower than in other European countries. (In France the figure is closer to 2.5 per 1,000. In Switzerland estimates range from 4 to 7 per 1,000.) Hard drug addiction in the United States is considerably higher. (Estimates range from 20 to 30 per 1,000.)[10]

Because many of the countries that have implemented drug legalization laws have had some success in controlling drug use and drug abuse, supporters of drug legalization in the United States believe that similar strategies should be implemented here. However, because there have been costs associated with these programs, including economic and social costs, opponents of legalization also use these programs as examples of what not to do.

Chapter 5

Legalization of Drugs: Reasons For

Over the years, groups have formed to change drug laws, especially for marijuana use. Supporters of legal marijuana use say it is no worse than tobacco or alcohol and that it has a legitimate medical value. The National Organization for the Reform of Marijuana Laws (NORML) sponsors grass roots campaigns such as "Honk If You Love Hemp" demonstrations. (Hemp is another word for marijuana.) The organization tries to make people aware of the widespread use of marijuana and tries to decrease fear of marijuana use. It works on behalf of people convicted under stringent drug possession laws. NORML has also filed lawsuits to force the federal government to conduct tests on the medical uses of marijuana.[1]

The Drug Reform Coordination Network is more concerned with how drug laws violate civil rights. It believes that current drug policy is "misguided" and costly. The group notes that of the four hundred thousand people in jail for drug crimes (one quarter of the entire prison population), many

*G*regory Porter, former executive director of NORML speaks at a "smoke-in" held in New York City's Washington Square Park.

have no previous criminal history. Three quarters of the people in prison for drug-related crimes are there for possession of drugs. More than 80 percent of the people arrested for drug crimes are arrested for personal use of a drug.[2]

In 1996 Californians for Compassionate Use, a group of pro-marijuana advocates, decided to sponsor California Proposition 215. This statute made it legal for people to use marijuana for medical conditions such as cancer, glaucoma, and AIDS. A similar law was also passed in Arizona.

Soon after, the federal government challenged these laws on the grounds that they were illegal. A judge disagreed, saying that states have a right to regulate drug use within their borders. However, these statutes are still being challenged by the federal government.[3]

Reasons for Drug Legalization

Supporters of drug legalization point to several reasons that drug use should be legalized—or at least decriminalized—in the United States. Supporters say that drug laws are prosecuted inconsistently, they corrupt law enforcement officials, create a criminal class, undermine respect for authority, cause crime, and restrict personal freedom. Other reasons, such as the medical value of some illegal drugs, also exist.

Drug Laws Make Drug Problems Worse

Supporters of legalization believe that the legal consequences of drug use actually make the problem worse. For instance, if an addict goes to jail (instead of a treatment center), he or she is further exposed to drug use and abuse since illegal drugs are often smuggled into prisons. Mandatory sentencing means a first-time user can go to jail for five or more years, which could easily turn a casual, one-time user into a hardened criminal. Also, drugs obtained illegally can be contaminated with additives, ranging from baking soda to rat poison, which can cause overdoses, illnesses, and even death. In addition, it is much less expensive to treat a person for drug abuse than it is to jail him or her. It costs around $37,500 to imprison a person for one year, whereas it costs $15,000 for an inpatient treatment program.[4]

Prosecution Is Inconsistent

Supporters of legalization believe that drug laws are inconsistent and unevenly prosecuted. For example, national attention has centered on the case of Will Foster, who was arrested for growing marijuana on his property in Tulsa, Oklahoma. He said that the marijuana was for personal use, to control pain related to arthritis. (Thirty-two states have passed statutes recognizing the medical uses of marijuana. Oklahoma is not one of them.) Foster was willing to plead guilty and save the government the cost of a

*M*embers of the group Californians for Compassionate Use march in support of legalizing marijuana for medical use.

jury trial in exchange for a reduced sentence. But his offer was rejected. In January 1997, he was sentenced to ninety-three years in prison and fined sixty-five thousand dollars. Observers who watched the case were stunned. The sentence this man received for growing a few marijuana plants was much more severe than the prison sentences some multiple murderers have received.[5]

Supporters of legalization also believe that drug laws are currently applied in a racist way. They find that African Americans and Hispanics are much more likely to receive mandatory minimum sentences than whites arrested for the same crimes.[6]

Drug Laws Corrupt Law Enforcement Officials

Supporters of legalization say that the current laws serve to corrupt police forces. Because there is so much money involved in drug dealing, law enforcement officers may be offered bribes. Sometimes they take these bribes. Inspectors who check luggage and packages at the border to prevent smuggling, called customs inspectors, have been convicted of taking bribes from drug traffickers. FBI agents, DEA agents, police officers, and prosecuting attorneys have all been convicted of bribery in drug-related cases. Most major cities have suffered from such scandals in recent years.

Since current drug laws allow the confiscation of property, accusations of drug use and possession can be used against people to take their property. Often, people only indirectly involved with drug possession or use find their property being taken. For example, the owner of a rental house can lose the house if a tenant is involved in a drug offense. This property is then used by drug enforcement officials in their jobs or auctioned to raise money for enforcement efforts. Critics contend that law enforcement officials misuse property confiscation laws. They also believe that these laws are unconstitutional.[7]

Drug Laws Create a Criminal Class

Supporters of drug legalization efforts say that drug laws create criminals. Keeping drugs illegal turns a large number of otherwise law-abiding citizens into criminals. Since this criminal class is enormous, numbering in the millions, and it is made up of

people from all walks of life, the police have to resort to desperate tactics to enforce laws. They spy on people, record their conversations, and trap citizens into buying from them during undercover operations.[8] Using such tactics to arrest otherwise law-abiding citizens causes everyone to be mistrustful and suspicious of the government.

*A*ctor Woody Harrelson is a strong advocate for legalizing industrial hemp, which does not contain the psychoactive properties of marijuana.

Drug Laws Undermine Respect for Authority

This widespread use of illegal drugs undermines respect for laws, supporters of legalization say. There are many laws against drug use, but people do not obey them. They learn not to take such laws seriously. This makes them more likely to have contempt for other laws and also for authority figures.

There is also concern over the hypocrisy of politicians and other lawmakers who talk about the need for strict drug laws when they admit to having used drugs themselves. This was evident when President Clinton ran for office and was asked whether he ever smoked marijuana. He admitted that he had done so. Later, when he called for stricter enforcement of drug laws, some people did not take him seriously.

Finally, many of the people who grew up in the 1960s and experimented with illegal drugs do not believe that they are as dangerous as is generally perceived. This makes it hard for some of them to support serious efforts to eradicate drug use especially if those efforts infringe on other rights, such as the right to privacy.[9]

Organized Crime Reaps Profits

Supporters of drug legalization also say that organized crime would lose its profit motive if drug use were legalized and regulated by the government. There would be much less profit in drug dealing. They point out that gangsters who controlled liquor distribution during the Prohibition Era corrupted law enforcement officials, terrified citizens, and made millions of dollars on the black market. Organized crime syndicates who transport and sell drugs engage in the very same acts.[10]

Drug Laws Cause Crime

Making drugs legal, supporters claim, would reduce other crimes as well. A great deal of violence occurs when gangs or organized crime groups try to protect their territory. Violence is used to solve disputes, because the court system obviously cannot be used.

Also, other crimes related to drug dealing would be reduced. For example, people who make money illegally have to hide where their money comes from. This activity is called money laundering, and it is a serious crime.

Further, the illegal drug trade is estimated to generate $100 billion a year. If some of that profit were taxed, as legal profits are, then treatment and prevention programs could easily be funded.

If drugs were legalized, the price would go down because dealers would not run the risk of going to jail and would not have to smuggle drugs into the country. Because users would have inexpensive drugs readily available, they would not need to turn to crime to support their habits.

If drug use were legal, supporters say, the drug trade would no longer need to involve children and teens. As it stands now, drug dealers often entice young people to work for them, because police officers are less suspicious of youth.[11]

Illegal Drugs Are No Worse Than Legal Drugs

Supporters of drug legalization say that many illegal drugs have the same effects as legal drugs. In particular, they claim that marijuana is less dangerous than tobacco because it is not as addictive. Supporters of drug legalization also believe that if people are expected to handle alcohol use, they can be expected to handle marijuana use. Although some people might have trouble using drugs without abusing them, the answer is not in banning these substances, but in providing education, prevention, and treatment programs for those who do develop problems associated with drug use.[12]

Drug Laws Restrict Personal Freedom

Supporters of legalizing drugs believe that current laws about drug use and abuse have seriously limited individual freedoms. For example, random drug testing of employees violates the right to privacy. Students are subject to more extensive invasions of their privacy. Some schools use drug-sniffing dogs; others carry out locker searches. Some require drug testing of all their students. The Supreme Court has ruled that these invasions of privacy are legal because students do not have the same rights as adults.

Supporters of legalization also feel that laws of forfeiture are unconstitutional. Laws allowing law enforcement officials to search the homes and automobiles of suspected users and dealers are criticized for being a form of illegal search and seizure. When people who possess a small amount of a drug are sentenced to greater prison terms than people who commit violent crimes, such as assault, rape, and murder, their right not to be subject to cruel and unusual punishment is violated.[13]

Drug Abuse Is a Medical and Social Problem

Supporters of legalizing drug use say that treating drug abuse as a medical and social problem will be more effective than treating it as a legal one. Putting more people in jail, they say, will not stop the problem. By better understanding what causes addiction, the medical community can help treat and cure addicts. By improving social ills—such as lack of education, lack of opportunity, and poverty—people will not feel the need to turn to drugs. If time and money are spent on addressing these issues, the quality of life for everyone will be greatly improved. By simply arresting people, the cause of the problem is never corrected and will never go away.[14]

Chapter 6

Legalization of Drugs: Reasons Against

In order to stop problems associated with drug use and abuse, groups such as the Partnership for a Drug-Free America and Drug Watch International have formed. They believe that drug abuse is such a serious problem that every effort must be made to combat it. This means legalization must be opposed, for a variety of reasons.

Costs of Drug Use

One of the main arguments opponents of legalization use is the high cost of drug use and abuse. They note that the economy suffers when users lose their jobs or when they make mistakes while working. They also put others at risk, especially if their occupations affect the health and safety of others, such as doctors, pilots, or bus drivers. Drug use also affects people's health. For example, inhalants can cause permanent brain damage. Cocaine can cause heart attacks. Pregnant women who use drugs can give birth to premature, brain-damaged, or drug-addicted babies. Economically, taxpayers must often bear the costs of health problems associated with drug use.[1]

Drug use can also cause personal problems such as the loss of friends and family. Users are more likely to abuse or neglect their children. They are also more likely to be involved in cases of domestic violence. Other personal problems result when users lose the motivation to do well in school, to go to college, or to find a good job.

All of these costs would still exist if drugs were made legal. By keeping drugs illegal, however, opponents believe fewer people suffer from these problems.

Tougher Drug Laws

When supporters of drug legalization say that drug laws have not worked, they often point out that the average sentence for drug-related convictions exceeds those for rape and manslaughter. Opponents of legalization maintain that even if drug laws have not worked as well as possible, they should not simply be abandoned. Some people believe that drug laws need to be even stricter, so that everyone will be strongly discouraged from using drugs. Some politicians have even called for the death penalty for drug dealers, saying that dealers should be held accountable for the injury and death they indirectly cause. Since opponents of drug legalization believe the human and economic costs of drug use are so great, they feel that even tougher laws may be necessary to stop drug use.

Enforcing Drug Laws

Supporters of legalization say that current drug laws undermine respect for authority. They say that

A law enforcement officer from a taskforce called CAMP (Campaign Against Marijuana Planting), carries a load of marijuana plants that were cut down during a raid near Ukiah, Utah.

because current drug policy has not stopped drug use, people just ignore the laws and, therefore, less respectful of all laws. Critics of legalization say that just because a law is ignored does not mean it should just be discarded. They point to the fact that although many people ignore speeding laws, those laws are not being abandoned. Critics of legalization say that drug laws—either current drug laws or tougher drug laws—need to be enforced. By giving the government and law enforcement agencies the necessary money to enforce the laws, people will have to obey them or will have to suffer the consequences. Increased enforcement will reduce the likelihood of people ignoring drug laws.

Critics of legalization also agree that sometimes drug laws are enforced inconsistently or unfairly. This, of course, is wrong. But they do not believe this is a good reason for legalization. Reform efforts should focus on prosecuting all crimes more fairly, not on doing away with some laws entirely.

The Right to Drug-Free Communities

Groups such as Drug Watch International perceive drug use as a major threat to all communities. This group, and others like it, promotes prevention and opposes efforts at legalization. They claim "effective prevention can take place only with positive societal norms which embrace and support healthy drug-free attitudes."[2] When supporters of legalization say that drug laws infringe on individual rights, Drug Watch International and other groups say that they support individual rights as long as those rights do not threaten "the stability, health and welfare of society."[3] They believe drug use is such a dangerous

••• 49 •••

problem that limiting personal freedoms is a small sacrifice to make. They say that people who are violating the law do not have a right to privacy. They believe that drug use is such a great threat that random drug testing and other controversial measures are needed. In addition, they say that laws of forfeiture ensure that people do not profit from the drug trade.

Supporters of drug legalization often note that adults have a right to do as they wish with their bodies. Critics of legalization say that this is not true. To take an extreme example, they point out that suicide is illegal everywhere in the country. Instead of allowing people to kill themselves when they are unhappy, critics say, society has a responsibility to help them solve their problems. Critics also point to frequently passed laws that restrict the rights of adults to do as they wish with their bodies, such as requiring all drivers and passengers in vehicles to wear seat belts and requiring motorcyclists and bicyclists to wear helmets. These laws protect people from themselves. Drug laws work in the same way.

Decriminalization Will Not Work

Supporters of decriminalizing drugs often believe decriminalization puts the focus of drug laws where it should be—on dealers and traffickers. Critics of decriminalization say that it does not work in the areas that have tried it, and it will not work in this country. Decriminalization does nothing to decrease the demand for drugs, they believe. If there are fewer penalties for personal use, more people might be inclined to use drugs more often, thereby increasing the problems associated with drug use.

Harm Reduction and Medicalization Cause Problems

Supporters of drug legalization often say that a certain number of people will have drug abuse problems whether or not drugs are legal, and they should be able to seek help without fear of punishment. These supporters believe that harm reduction, such as giving away free needles to heroin users, is a good approach. They also believe that medicalization—allowing physicians to prescribe doses of drugs to addicts—helps relieve some of the costs associated with drug abuse. Critics say this is not so. They believe that efforts at harm reduction and medicalization merely serve to encourage drug users and abusers. Critics say that drug abusers need treatment, but if they are not penalized for their behavior, they will not seek help. Critics believe that treatment should be provided to users who seek it, but they also believe that users who do not seek treatment, or who fail at their efforts to stop abusing drugs, should be punished.

No Medical Value

Many supporters of drug legalization say that some drugs, especially marijuana, have a medicinal value, and people should be able to use these drugs for medical reasons. Critics say that the medical value of marijuana and other illegal drugs is very small. They say that any of the medical properties of marijuana can be achieved with other legal drugs. They say that marijuana for medical use is just a way for people to use marijuana for recreational purposes.

Perceived Danger

Critics of drug legalization also claim that if drugs were legalized, people would believe that they were not dangerous. They feel that this is especially true in the case of teens, who are most susceptible to drug use. They fear that teens would reason, "if drugs were really that bad for you, they would be illegal." Thus, potential users would not be aware of the great risks of drug use and abuse.

Demand Will Increase

Critics of legalization say that legalization would increase drug use, just as legalizing alcohol at the end of Prohibition increased alcohol use. They believe that removing penalties for drug use will increase the demand for drugs. This increase would result in more drug abusers and greater profits for the drug dealers. They point to the huge profits alcohol and tobacco companies generate. Drug legalization would only make the profits of drug dealers legal. Even though such profits could be taxed, critics believe that other problems might result, such as smuggling to avoid taxation, although this has not happened in the case of alcohol.[4]

Crime Would Rise

Critics of legalization also say that crime would not be reduced. People would still commit crimes while under the influence of drugs. They would still need money to buy drugs. Even allowing doctors to prescribe illegal drugs would cause problems, they say. An addict could sell his or her prescribed drugs illegally on the black market. Because not all addicts would be willing to register as addicts, an illegal market would still exist. Also, because children and

Tobacco

- An estimated 64 million Americans smoke, including 4.5 million teenagers age twelve to seventeen.

- Young people age twelve to seventeen who currently smoke cigarettes are nine times more likely to use illegal drugs and sixteen times more likely to drink heavily than nonsmoking teens.

Source: The National Household Survey on Drug Abuse, conducted by the Substance Abuse and Mental Health Services Administration, 1997.

teens would not be allowed to purchase drugs, they would still form an illegal market for them. Teens tend to want to experiment with drug use. They often try to get tobacco and alcohol, even though it is illegal for them to do so. They would do the same if currently illegal drugs were made legal.

Even if a change in laws made drugs cheaper and easier to obtain so that drug users might not have to steal in order to support their habits, the use of drugs can be related to other crimes. Critics use alcohol-related crimes as an example. Alcohol use can impair judgment and reduce inhibitions and self-control. In addition to accidents that occur when people using alcohol drive, other crimes occur. Some crime experts believe that as many as two thirds of all homicides, one half of all assaults, and one quarter of rapes are alcohol-related.[5] They believe other drugs can

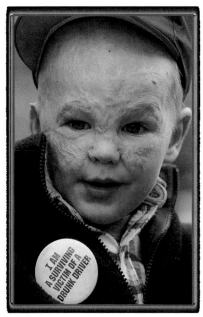

*G*eorge Harmon, age three, of Bridgewater, New Hampshire, was severely burned and his mother killed when their car was hit by a drunk driver.

cause this type of behavior as well. Allowing legal access to drugs would increase crime.

Consequences of Legal Drugs

When supporters of legalization note that adults have free access to tobacco and alcohol and that marijuana is no worse than tobacco, critics say that is exactly the point. Tobacco and alcohol are extremely dangerous and costly. Why, they ask, would we want to legalize similar drugs, knowing the costs to individuals and society?

Unknown Consequences

Critics of legalization also say that no one really knows what would happen if drugs were legalized; it is too dangerous to even try. The results could be disastrous for the entire society, and the risk should not be taken. Critics of drug legalization believe current drug policy and drug laws should be maintained or even strengthened.[6]

Community Anti-Drug Coalitions of America (CADCA)
901 North Pitt Street, Suite 300, Alexandria, VA 22314
(703) 706-0560
<www.cadca.org>

Drug Abuse Resistance Education (DARE)
P.O. Box 2090, Los Angeles, CA 90051-0090
(800) 223-3273
<www.dare-america.com>

Drug Information and Strategy Clearinghouse
P.O. Box 6424, Rockville, MD 20850
(800) 578-3472

Drug Policy Foundation (DPF)
4455 Connecticut Avenue NW, Suite B-500
Washington, DC 20008-2328
(202) 537-5005
<www.drugpolicy.org>

Inter-American Drug Information System
Organization of American States
1889 F Street NW, Room 845H, Washington, DC 20006
(202) 458-3809

National Clearinghouse for Alcohol and Drug Information (NCADI)
P.O. Box 2345, Rockville, MD 20847-2345
(800) 729-6686
<www.health.org>

National Inhalant Prevention Coalition (NIPC)
1201 West Sixth Street, Suite C-200, Austin, TX 78703
(800) 269-4237
<www.inhalants.org>

NORML
1001 Connecticut Avenue, NW, Suite 710
Washington, DC 20036
(202) 483-5500
<www.norml.org>

Partnership for a Drug-Free America
405 Lexington Avenue, Suite 1601, New York, NY 10174
(212) 922-1560
<www.drugfreeamerica.org>

Resource Center on Substance Abuse Prevention & Disability
1819 L Street, Suite 300
Washington, DC 20036
(202) 628-8080

Introduction

1. Tanya Kangas, "$20, Age 17, First Offense: Ten Years in Jail," *NORML News Archives*, January 22, 1998.

2. *1996 Survey of American Political Culture*, Gallup Organization and the University of Virginia, fact sheet (1996).

3. *ACE Fact Sheet on Higher Education*, American Council on Education, fact sheet (1997).

Chapter 1. Drugs of Abuse

1. David E. Larson, M.D., editor, *Mayo Clinic Family Health Book* (New York: William Morrow and Company, 1990), p. 439.

2. "Drug Use in the General U.S. Population," *1997 National Household Survey on Drug Abuse*, Substance Abuse and Mental Health Services Administration, United States Department of Health and Human Services, fact sheet (1997).

3. Larson, p. 434.

4. Ibid., p. 433.

5. Ibid., p. 443.

6. Ibid., p. 439.

7. "Special Report: Hockey's Little Helpers," *Sports Illustrated*, February 2, 1998, pp. 74–76.

8. Ibid., p. 76.

9. Eric A. Voth, M.D., "Drug Legalization, Harm Reduction and Drug Policy," *Annals of Internal Medicine* 123 (1995), pp. 461–465.

Chapter 2. History of Drugs and Drug Use

1. Dean Latimer and Jeff Goldberg, *Flowers in the Blood: The Story of Opium* (New York: Franklin Watts, 1981), p. 19.

2. David F. Musto, *The American Disease: Origins of Narcotic Control* (New York: Oxford University Press, 1987), p. 187.

3. Pure Food and Drug Act of 1906, Public Law 59-384.

4. Harrison Narcotics Act, Public Law 63–47.

5. Eric A. Voth, M.D., "Drug Legalization, Harm Reduction and Drug Policy," *Annals of Internal Medicine* 123 (1995), pp. 461–465.

6. Ibid.

Chapter 3. The War on Drugs

1. National Commission on Marijuana and Drug Abuse, Second Report, *Drug Use in America: Problem in Perspective*, Washington, D.C.: United States Government Printing Office, 1973.

2. Bernard Weintraub, "President Offers Strategy for United States on Drug Control," *The New York Times*, September 6, 1989, p. A1.

3. Jack B. Weinstein and Fred A. Bernstein, "The Unwarranted Denigration of Mens Rea on Drug Sentencing," *Federal Sentencing Reporter* 7:3 (Nov./Dec. 1994).

4. Weintraub, p. B7.

5. Jonathan Harris, *Drugged America* (New York: Four Winds Press, 1991), p. 149.

6. Partnership for a Drug-Free America, *Partnership Attitude Tracking Survey, 1998*. Key Findings, fact sheet (1998).

7. Weintraub, p. B7.

8. *Drug Data Summary 2*, Drugs and Crime Data Center and Clearinghouse, fact sheet (1994).

9. Joseph B. Treaster, "Police in New York Shift Drug Battle Away from Street," *The New York Times*, August 3, 1992, p. A1.

10. E. Wysong, R. Aniskiewicz, and D. Wright, "Truth and DARE: Tracking Drug Education to Graduation and as Symbolic Politics," Social Problems 41:3 (August 1994), pp. 448–472.

11. "Bill Bennett and Mario Cuomo Join Jim Burke as Co-Chairmen of Partnership for a Drug-Free America," press release (September 3, 1997), p. 3.

Chapter 4. Terms and Concepts of the Drug Legalization Debate

1. *Report and Recommendations of the Drug Policy Task Force*, New York County's Lawyers' Association, October 1996, p. 19.

2. Ibid., p. 20.

3. Ibid., p. 21.

4. *Drug Text International*, International Foundation on Drug Policy and Human Rights, database (1998).

5. Ibid.

6. Eric A. Voth, M.D., "Drug Legalization, Harm Reduction and Drug Policy," *Annals of Internal Medicine* 123 (1995), pp. 461–465.

7. *Drug Text International*.

8. Ibid.

9. *Drugs Policy in the Netherlands*, fact sheet 7, Cannabis Policy Update (1998).

10. *Commission Model for Action Plan (1995–1999)*, Commission of the European Communities (June 1994).

Chapter 5. Legalization of Drugs: Reasons For

1. National Organization for the Reform of Marijuana Laws (NORML), fact sheet (1998).

2. "A Guided Tour of the War on Drugs," Drug Reform Coordination Network, fact sheet (1998).

3. Californians for Compassionate Use, fact sheet (1997).

4. Jonathan Harris, *Drugged America* (New York: Four Winds Press, 1991), p. 155.

5. *Report and Recommendations of the Drug Policy Task Force*, p. 17.

6. Marc Mauer and Tracy Huling, "Young Black Americans and the Criminal Justice System: Five Years Later," The Sentencing Project, October 1995, p. 10. *Also*: The United States Sentencing Commission.

7. L. Grinspoon and J. Bakalar, "The War on Drugs: A Peace Proposal," *New England Journal of Medicine* 330, p. 357.

8. "A Guided Tour of the War on Drugs," p. 2.

9. Ibid.

10. James Ostrowski, "The Moral and Practical Case for Drug Legalization," *Hofstra Law Review* 18 (1990), p. 647.

11. Michael Z. Letwin, "Report from the Front Line: The Bennett Plan, Street-Level Drug Enforcement in New York City and the Legalization Debate," *Hofstra Law Review* 18 (1990), p. 896.

12. *Report and Recommendations of the Drug Policy Task Force*, p. 19.

13. Grinspoon, p. 357.

14. *Report and Recommendations of the Drug Policy Task Force*, p. 19.

Chapter 6. Legalization of Drugs: Reasons Against

1. Daniel Q. Haney, "Scientists Get a Look at the Brain on Drugs." Associated Press, January 14, 1998.

2. Drug Watch International, fact sheet (1998).

3. Ibid.

4. Eric A. Voth, M.D., "Drug Legalization, Harm Reduction and Drug Policy," *Annals of Internal Medicine* 123 (1995), pp. 461–465.

5. Ibid.

6. Ibid., p. 464.

acquired immunodeficiency syndrome (AIDS)—A deadly disease that is acquired by coming into contact with infected bodily fluids.

addict—A person who needs to use a drug.

addiction—The need to use a drug even after bad results or consequences.

alcohol—A depressant that can impair perception, motor skills, and judgment.

black market—The market for illegal goods.

caffeine—A mild stimulant found in chocolate, coffee, and some soft drinks.

casual user—A person who uses drugs recreationally, but only occasionally; not an addict.

controlled substances—Any drug or chemical that is illegal or requires a prescription to obtain.

decriminalization—Doing away with criminal prosecution for a crime.

dependency (physical)—A condition that occurs when the body relies on a drug and will have physical symptoms if the drug is no longer used.

dependency (psychological)—A condition that occurs when a person thinks he or she needs the drug to feel better and to get along.

depressants—Drugs that relax the body and reduce body functions.

designer drugs—Synthetic drugs made by people out of chemicals in homemade labs.

drug abuse—Using drugs, especially illegal drugs, in a harmful way, with loss of control over the drug use.

drug misuse—Using a drug for a reason other than its intended use.

ecstasy—A designer or synthetic drug that is a methamphetamine, a hallucinogen.

hard drugs—Illegal drugs that are considered to be the most dangerous and addictive, such as cocaine and heroin.

harm reduction—Measures that are used to prevent additional problems related to drug abuse.

heroin—A narcotic that is usually injected into a vein.

infectious disease—Any sickness that can be given from one person to another through contact of some sort.

inhalants—Chemicals that are sniffed to produce a high, such as Freon, glue, nail polish, or paint.

intravenous drugs (IV drugs)—Drugs injected directly into the bloodstream by using a needle.

legalization—Allowing people to use and possess drugs without legal consequences.

LSD (lysergic acid diethylamide)—A hallucinogen that can cause anxiety, exhilaration, confusion, even psychosis (loss of contact with reality).

marijuana—A drug that is smoked and that produces a sense of happiness and relaxation. It can also impair thinking, judgment, concentration, and physical coordination. Sometimes called hemp.

medicalization—Permitting doctors to prescribe illegal drugs to users already addicted to them in order to reduce dangers associated with drug abuse.

methadone—A synthetic drug similar to heroin that is used to treat heroin addiction.

methamphetamine—A hallucinogen that is made in a lab, such as the designer drug called Ecstasy.

morphine—A drug made from opium that is used to relieve pain.

narcotics—Drugs that relieve pain, cause numbness, and induce sleep.

opium—A drug made from the poppy plant, a narcotic that causes numbness and drowsiness.

organized crime—Rings, gangs, or groups of people who control different illegal activities, or illegal activities in certain areas.

over-the-counter drug—A drug that can be sold legally without a prescription.

PCP (phencyclidine)—A hallucinogen that can cause feelings of exhilaration, anxiety, and even psychosis (loss of contact with reality).

possession—Having any quantity of an illegal drug in your possession, such as in your locker, your room, your purse, or your pocket.

sedative—A drug used to relax the body and reduce body functions.

smuggling—To illegally bring something, such as drugs, into a country.

soft drugs—Illegal drugs that seem less dangerous and addictive than others; marijuana is an example of a soft drug.

stimulants—Drugs that excite or energize the body.

tobacco—A product whose main chemical, nicotine, is a stimulant; tobacco use can cause numerous health problems, including cancer.

tolerance—The need to use more of a drug to get the same effect.

trafficking—Bringing large quantities of drugs into the country and selling them illegally.

withdrawal symptoms—Physical and psychological symptoms that occur when a person stops using a drug; also used to describe the psychological effects addicts suffer from when they quit using a drug that causes psychological dependency.

zero tolerance—A policy under which the possession, use, or sale of any controlled substance is prosecuted, regardless of the amount of drug, the type of drug involved, or other circumstances.

Croft, Jennifer. *Drugs and the Legalization Debate*. New York: The Rosen Publishing Group, 1998.

Duke, Steven B., and Albert C. Gross. *America's Longest War: Rethinking Our Tragic Crusade Against Drugs*. New York: Jeremy Tarcher, 1993.

Johnson, Joan J. *America's War on Drugs*. New York: Franklin Watts, 1990.

Kuhn, Cynthia. *Buzzed: The Straight Facts About the Most Used and Abused Drugs From Alcohol to Ecstasy*. New York: W.W. Norton & Company, 1998.

Oliver, Marilyn Tower. *Drugs: Should They Be Legalized?* Springfield, N.J.: Enslow Publishers, Inc., 1996.

Schleichert, Elizabeth. *Marijuana*. Springfield, N.J.: Enslow Publishers, Inc., 1996.

Shulman, Jeffrey. *The Drug-Alert Dictionary and Resource Guide*. New York: Twenty-First Century Books, Inc., 1995.

Swisher, Karin L. *Legalizing Drugs*. San Diego: Greenhaven Press, Inc., 1996.

Thompson, Stephen, ed. *War on Drugs*. San Diego: Greenhaven Press, Inc., 1998.